AF480676

FROM PEAKS TO PALMS

A JOURNEY THROUGH INDIA'S NATURAL SPLENDOR

DR. MINAKSHI BANSAL

DEDICATION

This book is dedicated to the resilient spirit of India—a land of awe-inspiring landscapes and enduring traditions. To the guardians of its natural beauty and cultural heritage, who nurture and protect it for future generations. May the richness of this land continue to inspire and captivate us all.

❧❧❧

Contents

Contents

Prayer

This mantra is a prayer for universal well-being, invoking the blessings of various deities for protection, health, and happiness. It emphasizes the importance of experiencing the auspicious through all senses and living a life aligned with divine purpose. The repetition of "Shantih" at the end signifies a deep desire for peace in the individual, the environment, and the universe at large. This mantra is often recited as a prayer for peace, prosperity, and the physical and spiritual well-being of all beings.

༄༄༄

About The Author

Dr. Minakshi Bansal, born in the bustling metropolis of Delhi, India, has led a life steeped in artistry, scholarly pursuit, and an unwavering commitment to societal betterment. Following her marriage, she relocated to Ahmedabad, Gujarat, where she has since blossomed into a multifaceted beacon of inspiration for many. Dr. Minakshi is not only recognized as a gifted artist in the realm of Fine Arts but also as an esteemed author, a devoted social worker and a dedicated research scholar in Psychology. Her journey, marked by a profound dedication to elevating those around her, especially the downtrodden and underprivileged children of society, is a testament to her deep-seated belief in the transformative power of engagement and empathy.

From her earliest days, Minakshi was distinguished by an insatiable appetite for reading. Her literary universe was inhabited by characters and narratives that spanned ethical tales, motivational and inspirational stories, and the mythic parables imbued with life lessons. This voracious reading habit was not merely for personal edification but was driven by a desire to distill and disseminate the essence of these narratives to foster the development of students and peers alike. She was particularly captivated by the lives and teachings of historical figures and spiritual leaders such as Adi Shankaracharya, Swami Vivekananda, Dr. APJ Abdul Kalam, Mahamana Pandit Madan Mohan Malviya, Mahatma Gandhi, Sardar Vallabhai Patel, and Vinoba Bhave, among others. Their philosophies and life stories fueled her ambition to embody their ideals of resilience, selflessness, and relentless pursuit of knowledge.

Dr. Minakshi's academic and practical engagement with psychology has been equally noteworthy. As a research scholar, her focus has been on exploring the intricate tapestry of the human psyche, aiming to unlock the potential for psychological well-being and societal harmony. Her scholarly work is complemented by her active involvement in social work, where she employs her academic insights to make tangible differences in the lives of the underprivileged. Her endeavours in social work are characterized by an innovative approach that combines traditional wisdom with contemporary psychological practices to address the multifaceted challenges faced by these communities.

Her artistic talents, another facet of her diverse capabilities, are not merely a personal passion but also serve as a medium through which she communicates and connects with others. Her art, rich in symbolism and emotional depth, reflects her philosophical inquiries and social concerns, offering viewers a glimpse into the breadth of her intellect and the depth of her compassion.

In addition to her contributions to the arts and social sciences, Dr. Minakshi has embraced the healing arts of Pranic Healing, mastering the techniques developed by Master Choa Kok Sui. This practice, which focuses on the manipulation of Prana or life energy to heal the body and aura, has been both a personal journey of discovery and a means through which she extends her healing touch to others. Her proficiency in Pranic Healing is complemented by her advocacy and teaching of various forms of meditation aimed at rejuvenation, personal betterment, and the cultivation of harmony within individuals and communities alike.

Dr. Minakshi's life is a narrative of relentless pursuit, not just of personal achievement but of the upliftment and empowerment of society at large. Her diverse interests and talents—spanning the arts, literature, psychology, and the healing practices—converge on a singular path of service. She embodies the spirit of the luminaries who inspired her, channelling their legacy through her actions and teachings. Through her books, art, and social initiatives, she continues to inspire a new generation to embark on their own journeys of self-discovery, resilience, and altruism.

Her commitment to social betterment, particularly her focus on uplifting underprivileged children, reflects a deep understanding of the transformative potential of education and personal development. By integrating her knowledge of psychology, her artistic sensibilities, and her healing practices, Dr. Bansal has developed a holistic approach to social work that addresses both the immediate needs and the long-term well-being of the communities she serves.

As an author, Dr. Minakshi's writings offer a blend of inspirational insights, practical wisdom, and reflective contemplations drawn from her extensive reading and life experiences. Her books serve as a guide for those seeking to navigate the complexities of life with grace, resilience, and purpose. Through her narratives, she extends an invitation to her readers to explore the depths of their own potential and to contribute meaningfully to the collective well-being of society.

In Dr. Minakshi Bansal, we find a remarkable synthesis of the artist, the scholar, the healer, and the social activist. Her life's work stands as a beacon of hope and a source of inspiration for individuals seeking to make a difference in the world. Her story is a compelling reminder of the power of individual action, rooted in compassion and driven by a profound commitment to the betterment of humanity. Dr. Minakshi's legacy is not just in the tangible outcomes of her efforts but in the enduring spirit of inquiry, empathy, and service that she embodies.

ƿƿƿ

Preface

India, a land of startling contrasts and spectacular beauty, offers a journey as diverse as nature itself. From the snow-capped peaks of the Himalayas to the lush palm-fringed shores of the southern coast, the country unfolds a landscape rich with ecological and cultural diversity. This journey, a narrative exploration of India's natural splendor, traverses through its varied geographies—each region telling its own unique story of the earth's beauty and the human spirit's enduring connection to it.

Traveling through India is like turning the pages of a deeply engrossing novel, where each chapter reveals new characters, vistas, and tales. The starting point is often the majestic Himalayas in the north, where the mountains stand as sentinels to millennia of wisdom and tradition. These towering peaks hold secrets of the ages, sheltering not just diverse wildlife but also serving as spiritual havens for pilgrims seeking solace and enlightenment. As one descends into the plains, the narrative changes pace with the bustling towns and the serene rural landscapes that provide a backdrop to the rhythm of everyday life.

However, the true essence of India's natural diversity is best experienced through its heartlands and down into the lush greenery of its southern reaches. The forests and rivers of central India, such as those in Madhya Pradesh and Chhattisgarh, are less spoken of compared to the majestic mountains and serene coasts, but they are equally significant in the ecological and cultural narratives of the country. These regions are the guardians of biodiversity and are central to the conservation efforts that aim to balance human development with nature preservation.

Venturing further south, the Western Ghats present a dramatic interplay of mountainous terrain and verdant forests, creating an ecological barrier that influences the climate and agriculture of the region. The range is recognized as one of the world's eight 'hottest hotspots' of biological diversity, illustrating the intricate relationships between climate, geography, and life forms. The coffee plantations of Karnataka and the spice gardens of Kerala, nestled within these mountains, not only add to the state's economy but also enhance its cultural heritage, blending agricultural traditions with the natural environment.

No journey through India would be complete without a sojourn along its extensive coastline, which offers some of the most picturesque beaches in the world. From the vibrant shores of Goa to the spiritual tranquility of Tamil Nadu's coast, these areas serve as crucial habitats for marine life and are integral to the coastal communities whose cultures and livelihoods are inextricably linked to the sea.

This narrative journey culminates at the southernmost tip of the Indian subcontinent, Kanyakumari, where the Indian Ocean, Arabian Sea, and Bay of Bengal meet. This confluence is not just a geological wonder but also a symbol of the confluences that characterize much of India — where cultures, religions, and histories merge, creating a rich, complex tapestry that is continuously evolving.

Through this journey, one not only witnesses the sheer beauty of India's landscapes but also gains an insight into how deeply intertwined our lives are with the environment. Each region of India, with its unique ecological and cultural identity, contributes to the overall diversity of the nation, offering lessons on sustainability, coexistence, and respect for nature.

This exploration aims not only to celebrate the natural beauty of India but also to underscore the importance of conservation efforts. It highlights the need to preserve these landscapes not just for their aesthetic and ecological value but also for their cultural significance. The challenges faced by these regions—be it from climate change, urban expansion, or economic pressures—call for a thoughtful and sustained response to ensure that the splendors of India's nature are preserved for future generations.

In writing this narrative, the goal has been to capture the essence of India's natural environments and to convey the profound impact they have on the people who inhabit them. It is a personal reflection on the places that have not only shaped the cultural heritage of the nation but have also inspired countless visitors and locals alike. As we continue to navigate our relationship with the earth, may this journey through India's natural splendor serve as a reminder of the incredible beauty our planet offers and the collective responsibility we hold in safeguarding it.

ONE

Echoes of Kashmir - The Pristine Beauty and Saffron Trails

Kashmir, often heralded as a paradise on Earth, offers a breathtaking panorama that captivates the senses and calms the soul. Nestled in the northernmost part of India, this region is renowned not only for its stunning landscapes but also for its significant contributions to culinary and cultural heritage, particularly through saffron cultivation. The serene beauty of Kashmir is dramatically encapsulated by its majestic mountains, lush green valleys, and crystal-clear lakes, which reflect the sky like a mirror. These landscapes are not just a feast for the eyes but also a testament to the tranquil yet vibrant spirit of the region.

The journey through Kashmir's natural splendor begins with its rivers, which are lifelines that nourish the land and its traditions.

The Jhelum River, for instance, is not just a body of water but a cultural marker that flows through the valley, weaving together the stories and the livelihoods of the people who live along its banks. The river's course is a scenic adventure, bordered by poplars and weeping willows, creating a picturesque setting that embodies the tranquil and poetic essence of Kashmir.

Amidst these captivating landscapes flourishes the precious crop of saffron, known as the gold of Kashmir. Saffron cultivation in Kashmir is not merely an agricultural activity; it is a centuries-old tradition that involves meticulous labor and care. The town of Pampore, often referred to as the saffron town, becomes a hive of activity during the harvest season in autumn. The fields covered in purple saffron flowers are a sight to behold. Harvesting saffron is a delicate process that requires the stigmas to be plucked from the flowers at dawn, a task that has been preserved through generations. This spice not only flavors dishes but also colors the cultural fabric of Kashmir, used in both cuisine and traditional medicines.

The influence of saffron extends beyond the kitchens and apothecaries into the realms of religious and social celebrations, symbolizing purity and affluence. It is used in the preparation of special dishes during festivals and religious ceremonies, adding a layer of tradition to the gastronomical delights of Kashmir. The spice's warm hues and rich aroma encapsulate the essence of Kashmir, weaving it into the daily lives and celebrations of its people.

The pristine rivers and lush saffron fields of Kashmir offer more than just scenic beauty; they are a testament to the symbiotic relationship between nature and the cultural traditions of the region. This relationship supports not only the economy of Kashmir through tourism and agriculture but also preserves and promotes the cultural heritage that is intertwined with the natural environment. The serene waters and fertile lands are a constant source of inspiration and livelihood, making Kashmir a unique blend of natural beauty and cultural richness.

Thus, Kashmir stands as a beacon of natural beauty and cultural wealth, inviting travelers and explorers to witness its landscapes and partake in its rich traditions. The echoes of its rivers and the trails of its saffron fields continue to resonate, offering a timeless journey through the paradise that is Kashmir. As one traverses this enchanting region, it becomes clear that the beauty of Kashmir is not just in its landscapes but in the profound interactions between its natural endowments and the people who cherish and sustain them. This delicate balance of nature and culture is what makes Kashmir a truly special part of India, a land where every vista is a painting and every tradition a story.

"In the tranquil backwaters of Kerala, each paddle stroke tells a story of age-old rhythms and timeless beauty; here, nature whispers secrets of the deep to those who listen."

▷▷▷

TWO

PUNJAB: FIELDS OF GOLD AND RIVERS OF LIFE

Punjab, a region synonymous with vibrant culture and agricultural prosperity, is often referred to as the "Granary of India." This title is well-deserved, as Punjab plays a crucial role in the agricultural output of the nation, producing a significant percentage of India's wheat and rice. The state's name, Punjab, which means 'Land of Five Rivers,' is derived from the five major rivers that traverse its landscape: the Jhelum, Chenab, Ravi, Beas, and Sutlej. These rivers are not only the lifeline of Punjab's agriculture but also a central element of its cultural identity, shaping the economic and social fabric of the region.

The fertility of Punjab's soil and the bounty of its water resources make it an ideal place for agriculture. The extensive irrigation systems, developed over decades, harness the waters of the five rivers to cultivate vast fields of wheat, rice, and other crops. This agricultural abundance is visible in the endless stretches of verdant fields that dominate Punjab's landscape, often referred to as fields of gold when the crops ripen under the sun. The agricultural practices of Punjab not only feed millions within the state and across India but also support a variety of associated industries such as milling, farming equipment manufacturing, and food processing.

Beyond their economic importance, the rivers of Punjab hold significant cultural and religious value. They are considered sacred by many communities and play a pivotal role in the religious practices and daily lives of the Punjabi people. The rivers are venues for festive celebrations and spiritual gatherings, which draw thousands of devotees who partake in rituals and prayers. The intertwining of spiritual practices with daily life around these rivers reflects a harmonious balance between nature and human activity, a testament to the deep connection the people of Punjab have with their environment.

Moreover, the rivers are central to the folklore and literary expressions of Punjab. They are often personified in Punjabi literature and music, symbolizing both the joys and sorrows of life. These rivers have witnessed the history of Punjab, from the times of ancient civilizations through the colonial period, to the post-independence era, each phase leaving its imprint on the region. The historical events associated with these rivers are not just tales of the past but living memories that continue to influence the cultural consciousness of the people.

However, the relationship between Punjab and its rivers is not without challenges. Issues such as water pollution, riverbank erosion, and disputes over water sharing threaten the ecological balance and the livelihoods dependent on these waters. Efforts to manage these challenges involve a combination of traditional wisdom and modern technology, aiming to preserve the vitality of the rivers while meeting the needs of agriculture and human consumption.

The prosperity and challenges of Punjab are inextricably linked to its rivers and fields. The sustainable management of these resources is crucial for the continued well-being of the region. As Punjab moves forward, it faces the dual task of preserving its rich agricultural legacy and addressing the environmental concerns that impact its rivers and fields. This requires a collective effort from the government, local communities, and environmental organizations to ensure that Punjab can continue to be a land of abundance and cultural richness.

The essence of Punjab is captured in the life-giving waters of its rivers and the golden hues of its fields. The symbiosis between nature and culture in Punjab offers a model of how natural resources, when managed with respect and care, can sustain not just the physical needs of a population but also its cultural and spiritual aspirations. As Punjab navigates the complexities of modernity and tradition, its rivers and fields remain a source of life and inspiration, reminding us of the enduring power of nature in shaping human destiny.

ᭁᭁᭁ

"The Himalayas stand not just as mountains but as monuments to the spiritual quests of many; their peaks, cloaked in the serenity of the skies, reach towards the heavens as if in prayer."

▷▷▷

THREE

HIMACHAL PRADESH: AMONG THE CLOUDS AND ORCHARDS

Himachal Pradesh, often referred to as the "Abode of the Gods," offers a striking blend of breathtaking landscapes and profound spiritual allure. This northern Indian state is nestled amidst the towering Himalayas, home to some of the country's most scenic hill stations and expansive apple orchards. The beauty of Himachal Pradesh is not just in its serene landscapes but also in the deep cultural and spiritual connections that resonate through its mountains and valleys.

The journey through Himachal Pradesh is like traversing a living gallery of nature's artistry. The hill stations such as Shimla, Manali, and Dharamshala are not just popular tourist destinations but also cultural hotspots that offer a glimpse into the diverse lifestyles and traditions of the people living in the mountains. These towns, often perched at high altitudes, provide a retreat from the summer heat for visitors while offering panoramic views of snow-capped peaks, dense forests, and cascading waterfalls. The architecture here, with its quaint colonial influence and traditional Himachali elements, tells stories of a rich historical past intertwined with the natural environment.

Among these natural splendors, the apple orchards of Himachal Pradesh stand out as a testament to the region's agricultural prowess. The introduction of apples to Himachal Pradesh transformed the economic landscape of the region. Today, the state is one of India's major apple-producing regions, with orchards sprawling across its hills. The cultivation of apples involves the entire community; from planting and pruning to harvesting and marketing, each step is a community effort. The harvest season brings with it a festive atmosphere, as orchards become bustling hubs of activity. Families come together to pick apples, and the air is filled with the sweet fragrance of fresh fruit. This not only boosts the local economy but also fosters a strong sense of community among the residents.

The spiritual allure of Himachal Pradesh is deeply ingrained in its identity. The state is dotted with numerous temples and monasteries, making it a significant spiritual center for both Hinduism and Buddhism. These religious sites are often located in areas of exceptional natural beauty, suggesting a harmonious relationship between spirituality and nature. The famous temples like Jakhoo Temple in Shimla and the monasteries in Dharamshala serve as places of worship and pilgrimage, attracting thousands of devotees and tourists seeking spiritual solace and enlightenment. The rhythmic chants, the ringing of temple bells, and the serene settings provide a perfect backdrop for meditation and reflection.

Moreover, the hill stations of Himachal Pradesh have long been associated with tales of deities and spiritual legends, which are celebrated in local festivals and rituals. These cultural festivities are vibrant and colorful, reflecting the rich heritage of the region.

They provide an opportunity for visitors to witness the cultural amalgamation of music, dance, and storytelling, which encapsulates the spiritual and communal life of the people.

However, the increasing popularity of Himachal Pradesh as a tourist destination presents challenges such as environmental degradation and cultural dilution. The delicate ecosystems of the hill stations and the traditional ways of life are under threat from unchecked tourist activities and commercial exploitation. The need for sustainable tourism practices is crucial to preserve the natural beauty and cultural integrity of the region.

Efforts to promote eco-friendly tourism and local apple industries are essential in maintaining the ecological balance and supporting the local economy. These initiatives not only help in conservation efforts but also enhance the visitor experience, allowing tourists to enjoy the natural and cultural richness of Himachal Pradesh responsibly.

In essence, Himachal Pradesh is a land where the clouds meet the orchards, and spirituality mingles with natural beauty. The state offers a unique blend of tranquility, adventure, and spiritual awakening, making it a microcosm of the diverse cultural and natural heritage of India. As one explores the scenic landscapes and delves into the spiritual ambiance of the region, it becomes clear that Himachal Pradesh is not just a destination but a profound experience, a place where nature and human spirit connect in profound and enduring ways.

❧❧❧

"From the dense forests of Madhya Pradesh emerges
the melody of nature's untouched beauty; every leaf
and creature sings the song of the wild, unmarred
by time."

⊳⊳⊳

FOUR

UTTARAKHAND: SACRED PEAKS AND HEALING WATERS

Uttarakhand, revered as the 'Land of the Gods,' is a spiritual sanctuary nestled in the folds of the Himalayas in northern India. This state is celebrated not only for its raw, arresting beauty but also for its significant religious landmarks, particularly the Char Dham pilgrimage—comprising the sacred sites of Yamunotri, Gangotri, Kedarnath, and Badrinath. Each site possesses its own distinct spiritual aura and historical backstory, deeply embedded in Hindu mythology and practice. Additionally, Uttarakhand is blessed with numerous natural springs, which are believed to possess curative properties, drawing both pilgrims and health seekers to their soothing waters.

The Char Dham pilgrimage is an epitome of spiritual journey in India, attracting millions of devotees from across the globe. The pilgrimage begins at Yamunotri, dedicated to the Goddess Yamuna, and moves to Gangotri, which venerates Goddess Ganga. Both these places are sources of the sacred rivers Yamuna and Ganga respectively, and are deeply significant in Hinduism for their purifying and liberating powers. The journey continues to Kedarnath, home to one of the twelve Jyotirlingas of Lord Shiva, set against the backdrop of the majestic Himalayas. The final destination is Badrinath, where the temple of Lord Vishnu sits surrounded by towering peaks, often bathed in ethereal alpine glow. The arduous journey through these sacred sites is not merely a religious ritual but a transformative experience for believers, offering solace and a sense of spiritual renewal.

The trek to these holy sites is as physically demanding as it is spiritually uplifting. The paths wind through rugged terrains, dense forests, and along riverbanks, with the natural scenery providing a meditative backdrop. This pilgrimage is considered a journey of a lifetime, meant to purify the soul and offer salvation. The physical challenges of the journey intertwine with the spiritual quest, making the achievement of reaching each temple feel like a divine encounter. For many, the Char Dham is more than just temple visits; it is a way to connect with the divine through nature's magnificence.

Complementing the spiritual journey of the Char Dham, the natural springs scattered across Uttarakhand add another layer to the state's appeal. Places like Rishikesh and Haridwar are famed for their ghats and hot springs, which are frequented by visitors seeking spiritual cleansing and physical healing. The waters of these springs are rich in minerals and believed by many to cure ailments and restore health. This blend of spirituality and natural therapy draws a unique mix of pilgrims, tourists, and health enthusiasts, all looking to experience the sacred waters' reputed benefits.

These natural springs not only serve as centers for bathing rituals but are also integral to the local culture and daily rites. The act of immersing oneself in the holy waters, especially during religious festivals, is considered auspicious and is said to wash away one's sins. The serene ambiance of these springs, coupled with the chants and prayers echoing through the air, creates a profoundly peaceful and purifying experience. This ritualistic use of water exemplifies the deep-rooted belief in water's purifying power, which pervades many cultures and religions, particularly Hinduism.

However, the burgeoning influx of tourists and the environmental challenges posed by climate change are putting pressure on these fragile ecosystems. The need for sustainable management of both the pilgrimage routes and the natural springs is more urgent than ever to preserve these sacred and natural sites for future generations. Efforts are being made to regulate the flow of tourists, especially during peak pilgrimage seasons, and to implement eco-friendly practices that help maintain the ecological balance and spiritual sanctity of these areas.

Uttarakhand, with its blend of sacred peaks and healing waters, remains a testament to the profound spiritual heritage and natural beauty of India. The state not only offers a retreat for those seeking spiritual and physical wellness but also challenges the devout with its rigorous pilgrimages, making it a unique destination that offers both redemption and rejuvenation. As Uttarakhand continues to attract pilgrims and tourists alike, its stories of divine miracles and nature's wonders keep alive the centuries-old traditions and continue to inspire those who walk its sacred paths. This deep interconnection between the environment and spirituality in Uttarakhand highlights the intrinsic value of nature in human spiritual experiences, a reminder of the delicate balance we must maintain to preserve these ancient practices and places.

ᭁᭁᭁ

"The bustling spice markets of Mumbai are a carnival of aromas, where every scent tells a tale of ancient trade routes and the mingling of myriad cultures."

⊳⊳⊳

FIVE

DELHI: A CAPITAL BLEND OF HISTORY AND DIVERSITY

Delhi, the capital city of India, is a vibrant metropolis that embodies the spirit of India's past, present, and future. It is a city where history and modernity coexist in a dynamic tapestry of life. The city's landscape is dotted with centuries-old monuments, sprawling markets, and vast green spaces that offer respite from the urban sprawl. Delhi's unique character is defined by its cultural convergence, where diverse ethnic, religious, and social groups blend into a rich cultural mosaic.

At the heart of Delhi's historical narrative are its monuments—silent sentinels of the past, each telling a story of a bygone era. From the majestic Red Fort to the serene Humayun's Tomb, and from the towering Qutub Minar to the grand India Gate, these architectural marvels are not just tourist attractions but are pivotal chapters in the story of India. They are remnants of the Mughal, British, and earlier dynasties that shaped the city's identity. This historical richness offers a glimpse into the layers of influence that have contributed to the city's development over the centuries.

Beyond these monuments, the city's cultural fabric is woven through its bustling markets like Chandni Chowk, a thriving hub since the Mughal era, now a lively area where tradition and modernity collide. Here, one can savor the flavors of local cuisine, shop for traditional garments, or simply soak in the chaotic yet charming atmosphere. Similarly, areas like Khan Market, Hauz Khas, and Dilli Haat offer a blend of ethnic and contemporary shopping experiences, showcasing handicrafts from across India and serving global cuisines, thereby reflecting the city's cosmopolitan nature.

Delhi's cultural diversity is further accentuated by its festivals. Whether it's the colorful chaos of Diwali, the splendor of Eid, or the energetic dances of Baisakhi, every festival in Delhi is celebrated with fervor, reflecting the city's multi-ethnic makeup. These festivals not only offer a chance to celebrate traditions but also act as a bridge, bringing together people from different backgrounds, fostering a sense of community and mutual respect.

In contrast to the bustling city life, Delhi's green spaces provide a sanctuary of calm and beauty. The city is home to several well-maintained parks like Lodhi Gardens, where historical tombs stand amidst landscaped lawns and jogging tracks, and the Garden of Five Senses, a space designed to stimulate the senses and offer a leisurely escape from urban stress. The Delhi Ridge, an extension of the Aravalli range, serves as the city's green lung, hosting diverse flora and fauna and offering numerous trails for nature lovers and fitness enthusiasts. These green spaces are essential not only for ecological balance but also for providing Delhi's residents and visitors a place to rejuvenate.

Moreover, the integration of nature into urban planning is evident in the development of the Yamuna Biodiversity Park, which aims to restore the ecosystems along the banks of the polluted Yamuna river. Such initiatives highlight the city's growing environmental consciousness and its efforts to maintain sustainability amidst rapid urbanization.

The challenge for Delhi, however, lies in balancing this growth with the preservation of its cultural heritage and natural environment. Issues like air pollution, water scarcity, and congestion are stark reminders of the pressures that accompany urbanization. Addressing these issues requires innovative solutions that integrate traditional knowledge with modern technology, ensuring sustainable development while maintaining the cultural and historical integrity of the city.

Delhi's essence lies in its ability to adapt and evolve while preserving its heritage. It is a city that has witnessed empires rise and fall, each leaving behind legacies that are now woven into the fabric of its identity. As a melting pot of cultures, Delhi continues to draw people from across the nation and the world, each adding a strand to its ever-expanding cultural weave. The city's historical sites inspire awe and reflection, its markets pulse with life, its festivals dazzle with diversity, and its green spaces offer solace in the concrete jungle. In Delhi, the past and present merge seamlessly, creating a dynamic environment that is both challenging and exhilarating. As the city marches forward, it carries with it the rich tapestry of its diverse influences, standing as a testament to India's historical depth and its vibrant pluralism.

ppp

"Rajasthan's deserts whisper stories of valor; every grain of sand bathed in the setting sun recounts tales of Rajput glory and the enduring spirit of its people."

▷▷▷

SIX

THE HEART OF INDIA: MADHYA PRADESH'S NATURAL AND CULTURAL TAPESTRY

Madhya Pradesh, often referred to as the "Heart of India," not only because of its geographical location but also due to its rich cultural heritage and natural diversity, serves as a vibrant showcase of India's historical depth and ecological wealth. The state is a microcosm of the nation, presenting a blend of lush forests, bustling wildlife, and aromatic spice markets that offer a sensory feast to visitors and locals alike.

The natural landscape of Madhya Pradesh is dominated by expansive forests, which cover a significant portion of the state. These forests are not monolithic but are instead a mosaic of different ecosystems, ranging from the dense sal forests of the east to the dry deciduous forests of the north and west. These vast green expanses are vital to the ecological balance of the region and serve as the lung spaces of the central Indian plateau.

They are also home to some of India's best-known national parks and wildlife sanctuaries, including Bandhavgarh, Kanha, and Pench. These parks are celebrated not just for their biodiversity but also for being the habitat of the majestic Bengal tiger, an emblematic figure of India's wildlife conservation efforts.

The experience of exploring these national parks is transformative, combining the thrill of adventure with the serenity of being in nature's lap. Safari rides at dawn and dusk offer glimpses of the tiger in its natural habitat, alongside other fauna such as leopards, wild boars, and a variety of deer. The avian life in these forests adds a colorful and melodious layer to the experience, with numerous species of birds filling the canopy with their calls.

The forests of Madhya Pradesh also play a crucial role in the lives of many tribal communities who have lived in harmony with this environment for centuries. Their traditional knowledge of flora and fauna contributes significantly to conservation efforts and offers valuable lessons in sustainable living.

Apart from its natural beauty, Madhya Pradesh is also renowned for its spice markets, which are a vital part of the state's culinary heritage. Towns like Neemuch and Bhopal host vibrant spice markets that draw not only locals but also chefs and culinary enthusiasts from across the country.

Walking through these markets is an aromatic journey; stalls brim with locally grown spices such as coriander, turmeric, and chili, along with a variety of blends that are essential to the region's cuisine. These markets are more than just commercial hubs; they are cultural landmarks where traditional practices meet modern commerce. The interaction between vendors and buyers, negotiations over prices, and the exchange of recipes and culinary tips paint a lively picture of the local lifestyle.

The significance of spices extends beyond their culinary use; they are intertwined with the health and medicinal traditions of the region. Ayurveda, the ancient Indian science of life and wellness, utilizes these spices in various treatments, recognizing their healing properties and their role in maintaining a healthy lifestyle. This traditional knowledge is passed down through generations and is an integral part of the cultural fabric of Madhya Pradesh.

Cultural festivals in Madhya Pradesh also reflect the state's rich heritage, with many celebrations centered around harvests, seasons, and religious myths. These festivals are not only occasions for joy and community bonding but also times when the state's artistic expressions come to the forefront.

Dance forms like the vigorous Gudum Baja of the Baiga tribes or the graceful Matki dance are performed, and traditional crafts are showcased, providing insights into the region's diverse cultural expressions.

However, the challenges of conservation and development loom large over Madhya Pradesh. The pressure to modernize while preserving the natural and cultural heritage is palpable. Initiatives aimed at promoting eco-tourism and sustainable agricultural practices are being implemented, striving to balance economic growth with environmental stewardship. The state's approach to these challenges is crucial for its future, aiming to protect its natural resources while fostering a vibrant economy.

Madhya Pradesh, with its forests, wildlife, and spice-filled air, offers a unique journey through the heart of India. It is a place where nature and culture intertwine seamlessly, offering stories of survival, revival, and existential beauty. The state not only preserves its past but also embraces the future, making it a significant cultural and ecological haven in India's vast landscape.

As Madhya Pradesh continues to navigate the complexities of conservation and development, its heart beats strong—pulsating with the rhythms of its forests, the roars of its tigers, and the scents of its spice markets.

ᐁᐁᐁ

"The Western Ghats are not merely ridges of rock but the very spine of India's ecological diversity, supporting life in forms as varied as the colors at dawn."

▷▷▷

SEVEN

GUJARAT: LAND OF LEGENDS AND LUMINOUS LANDSCAPES

Gujarat, a vibrant state in the western part of India, is a land steeped in history, flavored with an abundance of spices, and adorned with diverse landscapes. From the arid expanses of Kutch to the lush greenery of the Gir forest, from the bustling city life of Ahmedabad to the tranquil beaches of Mandvi, Gujarat embodies a unique blend of tradition and modernity, nature and culture, calm and vibrancy.

The cultural richness of Gujarat is a testament to the centuries-old civilizations that flourished here, notably the Indus Valley Civilization with its major sites like Dholavira and Lothal, which provide crucial insights into ancient urban planning and maritime trade. Today, this historical depth is reflected in the state's numerous festivals, traditions, and architectural wonders. Gujarat is the birthplace of Mahatma Gandhi, the father of the nation, whose legacy in the state is immortalized by the Sabarmati Ashram in Ahmedabad. This connection infuses the state with a spirit of peace and non-violence, resonating through its culture and people's lifestyles.

Gujarat's festivals are vibrant tapestries of dance, music, and colors, with Navratri being the most celebrated, transforming nights into spectacles of dance and devotion. During Navratri, the entire state vibrates with the rhythms of the Garba dance, where men and women, dressed in colorful traditional attire, dance in circles with graceful movements and clapping hands. This festival not only reflects the state's rich cultural heritage but also its community spirit and the importance of traditions in binding people together.

The architectural grandeur of Gujarat is yet another facet of its cultural richness. The state is home to the UNESCO World Heritage Site of Rani ki Vav in Patan, a splendid example of ancient water storage systems, and the Sun Temple at Modhera, which is an architectural marvel of ancient solar alignment. The stepwells, palaces, and temples across Gujarat not only showcase exquisite craftsmanship but also tell tales of the state's glorious past and its ability to blend functionality with aesthetic beauty.

Gujarat's coastal beauty is as diverse as it is picturesque. With a coastline extending over 1,600 kilometers, it is the longest in India, featuring a variety of beaches and ports. The serene beaches of Mandvi and Diu offer tranquil retreats from the hustle of city life, while the bustling ports like Kandla and Mundra illustrate the dynamic trade activities that have historically made Gujarat a maritime powerhouse. These coastal areas are not just recreational spots but also hubs of economic activity and cultural exchange, reflecting the state's strategic importance in national and international trade networks.

The culinary spices of Gujarat add another layer to its cultural tapestry. Gujarati cuisine is renowned for its distinct flavors, which are both subtle and robust, sweet and spicy. Dishes like Dhokla,

Khakhra, and Thepla are not just food items but represent the state's culinary innovation, using local ingredients and spices in ways that are both delightful and surprising. The use of spices like mustard seeds, fenugreek, and asafoetida in Gujarati cuisine is not only for flavor but also for their digestive and nutritional benefits, showcasing a deep understanding of food as both sustenance and medicine.

Moreover, the spice markets of Gujarat are as vibrant as they are aromatic. Walking through these markets, one is enveloped by the scents of various spices, each telling its own story of journeys, trades, and culinary uses. These markets are central to the daily lives of the people, serving as places where tradition meets trade and where the old ways blend seamlessly with new demands.

However, maintaining the balance between preserving natural beauty, cultural heritage, and fostering economic growth poses a significant challenge for Gujarat. As it strides forward, the state faces the task of managing its resources sustainably, ensuring that its development does not come at the cost of its environmental or cultural treasures.

Gujarat is a microcosm of India's diversity and dynamism. With its rich history, vibrant cultural festivals, breathtaking architectural sites, extensive coastlines, and flavorful cuisine, Gujarat offers a unique blend of experiences that are deeply rooted in tradition yet vibrant with contemporary relevance. As one explores Gujarat, from its legendary landscapes to its luminous horizons, it becomes clear that this state is not just a place on the map but a living, breathing mosaic of life's colors.

"In Goa, the sands remember every wave, just as the shores recall every tide, capturing the essence of both transient visitors and the eternal sea."

ᐅᐅᐅ

EIGHT

RAJASTHAN: DUNES, FORTS, AND FLAVORS

Rajasthan, the land of kings and colors, is a vivid tapestry of arid deserts, grand forts, and rich flavors. It is a region that epitomizes the royal heritage of India, with its palatial complexes, gallant history, and vibrant cultural life. Each city in Rajasthan tells its own tale of heroism and beauty, set against the backdrop of the stark Thar Desert which extends its golden sands across the northwest of India.

The deserts of Rajasthan are not merely arid wastelands; they are alive with activity, culture, and biodiversity. The Thar Desert, also known as the Great Indian Desert, covers a significant part of Rajasthan, providing a landscape that is both challenging and enchanting. This desert is home to a variety of flora and fauna adapted to the harsh environment, including the resilient Khejri trees and the elusive Indian wild ass. The desert also supports a rich tapestry of human life, demonstrated in the vibrant culture of the local communities such as the Bishnois, who are known for their deep commitment to environmental conservation, and the Rajputs,

renowned for their valor and chivalry.

Rajasthan's historical architecture is a cornerstone of its allure, encapsulating the pomp and splendor of its bygone eras. The forts of Rajasthan, such as the majestic Mehrangarh Fort in Jodhpur, the Amer Fort near Jaipur, and the Kumbhalgarh Fort, are not just tourist destinations but symbols of Rajasthan's rich historical narrative. These forts, built on strategic locations atop hills or amidst deserts, were not only defensive structures but also residences of the royalty. Inside their imposing walls, elaborate palaces, courtyards, and temples tell stories of a feudal past filled with intrigue, opulence, and artistry. The architectural techniques and materials used in these structures reflect the ingenuity of their builders, who managed to create robust defenses as well as magnificent abodes in the challenging desert environment.

Beyond the forts, the palaces of Rajasthan are equally compelling. The City Palace in Udaipur, with its series of courtyards, pavilions, terraces, corridors, and gardens, is a classic example of the fusion of Rajput and Mughal architectural styles. The Lake Palace, also in Udaipur, appears to float magically on the surface of Lake Pichola, its white marble walls reflecting in the still waters of the lake, creating a dreamlike vista that has captivated the imaginations of travelers for centuries.

The flavors of Rajasthan's cuisine are as bold and spirited as its history and landscapes. Rajasthani food is a feast for the senses, characterized by its spicy curries and mouth-watering sweets. The arid climate and scarcity of water have influenced the local cuisine in unique ways, leading to the predominance of dishes that can last for several days and do not require reheating. Dishes like Ker Sangri and Gatte ki Sabzi are examples of this, made from dried ingredients that are rehydrated and cooked with yogurt and spices to create rich, flavorful meals. The iconic Dal Bati Churma, a combination of spicy dal, baked bati, and sweet churma, is a staple that exemplifies the heartiness of Rajasthani food.

Rajasthani cuisine also includes a variety of chutneys made from local herbs and spices like mint, garlic, and turmeric, which not only enhance the flavors but also offer health benefits suited to the desert environment. Sweets such as Ghewar, a disc-shaped sweet cake soaked in sugar syrup, provide a delightful end to a Rajasthani meal, reflecting the state's penchant for celebrating life with sweetness despite the harsh living conditions.

Rajasthan's cultural festivities, such as the Pushkar Camel Fair and the Desert Festival of Jaisalmer, showcase its traditions, crafts, and arts. These festivals, set against the dramatic landscape of the desert, are a riot of color and energy, featuring camel races, folk dances, and music performances, drawing visitors from across the world.

However, the challenges of conserving the cultural and natural heritage of Rajasthan in the face of modernization and climate change are significant. Efforts to maintain the architectural integrity of historical sites and to sustain the traditional lifestyles that thrive in its deserts are ongoing. Sustainable tourism and heritage conservation initiatives are vital to ensuring that the grandeur and spirit of Rajasthan can be passed down to future generations.

Rajasthan is a land where history, culture, and nature converge in a vibrant mosaic of experiences. From the rolling dunes to the towering forts and the spicy richness of its cuisine, Rajasthan offers a journey through time, showcasing the enduring spirit and resilience of its people. As one traverses this royal land, each scene and flavor builds upon the last to create a comprehensive picture of Rajasthan's majestic legacy.

ppp

"Tamil Nadu's temples are the custodians of silence,
their stones steeped in devotion, bearing witness to
centuries of prayer and the footfalls of pilgrims."

❧❧❧

NINE

UTTAR PRADESH: THE RIVERFRONT OF RELIGIOSITY

Uttar Pradesh, nestled in the heart of India, is a region that epitomizes the spiritual core of the nation. This vast state, with its rich tapestry of history, culture, and religion, is significantly shaped by the sacred river Ganges, which flows through it, offering both physical sustenance and spiritual salvation. The river is not just a water body but a cultural and spiritual symbol, deeply intertwined with the life and beliefs of the people. Along its banks, myriad festivals and rituals unfold, each illustrating the profound cultural significance of the Ganges in the daily lives and spiritual practices of the residents.

The Ganges in Uttar Pradesh is more than just a river; it is considered a goddess, and her waters are believed to purify the soul and grant moksha, or liberation. This belief is deeply ingrained in Hindu mythology and is vividly celebrated in numerous festivals throughout the year. The most prominent of these is the Kumbh Mela, held every twelve years at Prayagraj, where the Ganges meets the Yamuna and the mythical Sarasvati rivers. This festival is one of the largest religious gatherings in the world, drawing millions of pilgrims from across India and the globe. They come to bathe in the sacred waters, a ritual believed to cleanse them of sins and bring divine blessings.

Apart from the Kumbh Mela, numerous other festivals revolve around the Ganges, including the Ganga Dussehra, which celebrates the river's descent to the earth. During this festival, towns and cities along the riverbank come alive with devotional music, dance, and the glow of numerous lamps floated on the river in the evening. These lamps, set adrift in small boats made of leaves and flowers, create a mesmerizing spectacle of light dancing on the water, symbolizing the lifting of spiritual darkness and the guiding of souls towards enlightenment.

Varanasi, one of the world's oldest continually inhabited cities and a pivotal site in Uttar Pradesh, epitomizes the spiritual and cultural centrality of the Ganges. Here, the ghats—broad steps leading down to the river—are perennially thronged with pilgrims performing rituals, bathing, and conducting funeral rites. The evening aarti at Dashashwamedh Ghat is a particularly profound tribute to the river, involving elaborate rituals performed by priests to the accompaniment of bells and songs. This ritual captures the deep reverence the locals hold for the Ganges, treating her not only as a giver of life but also as a divine entity deserving of worship.

The river also supports a rich tapestry of artistic expression. Classical music, dance forms like Kathak, and various folk arts in Uttar Pradesh have often drawn inspiration from the life along the Ganges. These art forms narrate stories of the river, its myths, and its people, further embedding the Ganges into the cultural identity of the region. Literary works in Hindi and other regional languages frequently reference the river, illustrating its role as a source of both poetic inspiration and existential reflection.

However, the relationship between the people and the Ganges is not solely spiritual; it is also practical. The river is a crucial resource for agriculture, which is the backbone of Uttar Pradesh's economy. The fertile plains along the riverbanks are cultivated for multiple crops annually, supporting millions of livelihoods. Furthermore, the river sustains a variety of ecosystems and a biodiversity that is essential for the environmental health of the region.

Yet, the Ganges faces significant challenges, including pollution from industrial waste, agricultural runoff, and human activities. Efforts to clean and preserve the river are ongoing, involving government initiatives and local community actions, reflecting the crucial need to balance ecological health with cultural practices and economic activities.

The Ganges in Uttar Pradesh is a powerful symbol of spirituality, culture, and life. Its waters reflect the skies and the flickering lights of countless lamps during festivals, but they also mirror the challenges of contemporary life in a rapidly modernizing society. The riverfront of Uttar Pradesh, with its bustling ghats, solemn rituals, and vibrant festivals, offers a unique insight into the interplay between nature and humanity, between ancient traditions and modern imperatives. As the state looks towards the future, the enduring presence of the Ganges serves as a reminder of the need to cherish and preserve this vital and sacred resource that has shaped the cultural and spiritual contours of Indian civilization for millennia.

ᐅᐅᐅ

*"Kanyakumari's waters, where three seas meet,
reflect the confluence of histories, cultures, and
souls, converging at India's southernmost tip."*

ᗷᗷᗷ

TEN
BIHAR: THE ANCIENT ECHOES AND MYSTIC RIVERS

Bihar, a state rich in historical and spiritual heritage, stands as a testament to India's ancient civilization and cultural depth. Situated along the sacred Ganges River, which flows through the heart of the state, Bihar is a land where history resonates through ages-old ruins and spiritual sites. From the ruins of Nalanda University to the sacred city of Bodh Gaya, the region's mystic rivers, primarily the Ganges, have witnessed the unfolding of significant historical and spiritual narratives that have shaped not only the state but also the broader Indian subcontinent.

The Ganges in Bihar is more than just a river; it is a lifeline that has nurtured civilizations and inspired countless generations through its spiritual significance. As it meanders through the state, the Ganges touches numerous sites that are steeped in historical and religious importance. One of the most profound of these is Bodh Gaya, where Prince Siddhartha attained enlightenment under a Bodhi tree and became Buddha. This small town, now a major pilgrimage site for Buddhists from around the world, hosts the magnificent Mahabodhi Temple, a UNESCO World Heritage site, which stands as a profound marker of divine presence and human devotion. The temple, with its soaring spire, is a sanctuary of peace, drawing visitors who seek spiritual solace and wisdom.

Further along the river is Patna, the capital of Bihar, where ancient Pataliputra once stood. This city, once a seat of power for various Indian dynasties, including the Mauryan and Gupta empires, today hosts several historical sites that echo the past's grandeur. The Patna Museum houses artifacts that span thousands of years, providing insights into the rich tapestry of Bihar's history. Near Patna, the site of the ancient university of Nalanda lies in ruins, yet it continues to be a symbol of the scholarly excellence that characterized ancient India. Nalanda was an intellectual hub that attracted scholars from various parts of the world, a place where knowledge transcended physical boundaries and cultural divides.

Apart from these globally renowned sites, Bihar is dotted with numerous lesser-known but equally significant spiritual sites along the Ganges. Places like Sultanganj, where the river's holy waters are believed to turn northward, are considered auspicious and attract devotees year-round. The Ganges here is said to have the power to cleanse sins and grant moksha, or liberation from the cycle of life and death, which makes it a frequent site for spiritual baths and rites.

The festivals along the Ganges in Bihar are vibrant and deeply spiritual. Chhath Puja, a festival unique to Bihar and the adjoining regions, is an ode to the sun god, Surya, and his sister Chhathi Maiya, who is believed to grant the wishes of those who partake in the rigorous rituals. During the festival, devotees gather along the banks of the Ganges and other rivers to offer prayers, perform rituals, and make offerings to the sun at dawn and dusk. The riverbanks are lit with earthen lamps, and the air resonates with folk songs and prayers, creating a mesmerizing atmosphere that strengthens community bonds and reaffirms faith in divine powers.

The rivers of Bihar, particularly the Ganges, are not only spiritual sanctuaries but also vital to the state's agriculture. The fertile plains along the riverbanks support the cultivation of rice, wheat, and various other crops, sustaining the local economy and feeding millions. However, like many of India's rivers, the Ganges here faces threats from pollution and environmental degradation, which affect both the river's health and the people who depend on it.

Efforts to preserve and clean the river have been initiated, but the challenge remains daunting. Balancing the needs of conservation with the necessities of a growing population and a developing state is complex. The river, with its historical significance and spiritual sanctity, demands a collective commitment to sustainability and reverence that transcends mere economic considerations.

Bihar's mystic rivers, especially the Ganges, are central to its identity. They are threads that weave through the fabric of the state's history, spirituality, and everyday life. The ancient echoes of Bihar's riverside civilizations and the continuous flow of its waters tell a story of endurance and adaptation. As Bihar continues to evolve, the enduring presence of the Ganges serves as a reminder of the state's ancient legacy and its ongoing journey towards spiritual and material prosperity. The river, revered and vibrant, continues to be a symbol of life and continuity in the heart of Bihar, resonating with the ancient echoes of a land enriched by history and spirituality.

ᖫᖫᖫ

"The lush tea gardens of Assam are not just landscapes but the lifelines of tradition, where every leaf holds a flavor steeped in the legacy of the land."

❦❦❦

ELEVEN

WEST BENGAL: THE TIDES OF TRADITION

West Bengal, a state in eastern India, is a tapestry of vibrant cultures, rich histories, and natural beauty, woven together by the threads of tradition and modernity. The state stretches from the Himalayas in the north, with its lush tea gardens, to the fertile plains of the south, cradled by the mighty Hooghly River. This river, a distributary of the Ganges, not only nurtures the land but also carries with it centuries of cultural heritage, making West Bengal a unique blend of the past and the present.

The cultural richness of West Bengal is epitomized in its capital, Kolkata, historically known as Calcutta. This city, once the capital of British India, is often referred to as the "Cultural Capital of India" due to its prolific contributions to literature, arts, and music. Kolkata has been home to some of India's most revered figures, such as Rabindranath Tagore, whose writings resonate with the spirit of Indian identity and universal humanism. The city's architectural heritage, from the grand colonial structures along the Maidan area to the iconic Howrah Bridge that spans the Hooghly River, reflects a history of artistic and architectural influences from around the globe.

Festivals in West Bengal are grand and colorful, particularly Durga Puja, the most celebrated event across the state. This festival, dedicated to the goddess Durga, is a social and cultural phenomenon that transforms the entire state into a vibrant tableau of art, music, and spiritual fervor. Artisans create elaborate clay models of the goddess, which are worshipped for five days with great pomp and show before being immersed in the waters of the Hooghly River, symbolizing the cycle of birth and rebirth. The festival is not only a religious occasion but also a celebration of artistic expression, community, and Bengali culture.

Beyond the bustling cities, the northern reaches of West Bengal house the verdant Darjeeling and Dooars tea gardens. These tea gardens are not merely agricultural lands; they are part of the cultural and economic fabric of the region. Darjeeling tea, known globally for its aroma and quality, is cultivated in the slopes of the Himalayas, where the cool climate and rich soil contribute to its unique flavor. The tea estates themselves are places of natural beauty, offering serene landscapes that are a stark contrast to the urban environment of the cities.

The role of the Hooghly River in the life of West Bengal cannot be overstated. Flowing through the heart of the state, it is a source of economic sustenance, a waterway that supports commerce and transport. The riverbanks host many small towns and villages where traditions of fishery and trade flourish. The ghats, or riverbanks, are lively places where daily life unfolds with a rhythm dictated by the river. People gather here not only for daily chores but for rituals and celebrations, making the river a central element in the community's social and religious life.

Moreover, the cultural activities along the Hooghly River are a testament to the state's rich literary and artistic traditions. Kolkata's annual book fair and numerous cultural festivals along the riverbanks are significant events that attract intellectuals, artists, and tourists alike. These events are platforms for debates, literary discussions, and cultural exchanges that reflect the intellectual vibrancy of the state.

However, the juxtaposition of tradition and modernity in West Bengal is also a source of challenges. The pressures of urbanization, pollution, and economic changes threaten the natural and cultural heritage of the state, including the health of the Hooghly River and the sustainability of the tea gardens. Efforts to balance these pressures with the need to preserve the cultural identity and environmental integrity of West Bengal are ongoing.

West Bengal is a state where the past and the present coexist in a dynamic relationship. The Hooghly River and the tea gardens are not just physical entities but symbols of the state's heritage and its ongoing story. From the literary streets of Kolkata to the spiritual serenity of the river ghats, from the lush greenery of the tea gardens to the festive fervor that grips the state during Durga Puja, West Bengal offers a unique glimpse into the soul of India. It is a place where tradition is not just remembered but celebrated, where culture thrives not in isolation but as a part of everyday life. As West Bengal continues to navigate the tides of change, it remains a vibrant testament to the enduring spirit and rich tapestry of Indian culture.

ᑭᑭᑭ

"Sikkim's commitment to organic farming is a testament to the harmony between man and nature; it is where each seed planted is a promise to the earth."

ᗺᗺᗺ

TWELVE

SIKKIM: THE ORGANIC STATE WITH HEAVENLY VISTAS

Sikkim, a small but splendid state nestled in the northeastern part of India, is a region where the majesty of nature is in profound harmony with sustainable agricultural practices. Known for its commitment to organic farming, Sikkim has distinguished itself as the first fully organic state in India, a testament to its dedication to environmental consciousness and sustainable development. The state's landscapes, ranging from lush subtropical woodlands in the south to the alpine zones in the north, offer breathtaking vistas that are not just visually stunning but also ecologically diverse.

The journey of Sikkim towards becoming an organic state began in earnest in 2003, with a visionary policy that aimed to transform the agricultural sector. This shift was driven by a recognition of the inherent value of preserving the natural beauty and biodiversity of the region, which is critical given its location in the Himalayas. The implementation of organic practices involved phasing out chemical fertilizers and pesticides and promoting organic certification for all agricultural produce. By 2016, Sikkim was officially declared free from chemical pesticides and fertilizers, making it a pioneering model of organic farming globally.

This commitment to organic farming in Sikkim is more than an agricultural policy; it is a philosophy that permeates the lives of its people and the management of its resources. The impact of this shift is manifold, benefiting not only the ecological balance but also the health and livelihoods of the local population. Farmers in Sikkim engage in the cultivation of a variety of crops that are adapted to the region's micro-climates, including cardamom, ginger, turmeric, and a range of fruits and vegetables. These organically grown products are highly valued not just within India but also in international markets, enhancing the economic welfare of the farming communities.

Moreover, Sikkim's approach to tourism is deeply influenced by its organic ethos. Visitors to the state can explore its organic farms, participate in responsible trekking expeditions, and enjoy local cuisine that is both delicious and sustainably produced. The integration of organic farming with eco-tourism has created a unique brand for Sikkim, attracting tourists who are environmentally conscious and keen to experience the purity of nature.

The natural beauty of Sikkim is as varied as it is enchanting. The state offers some of the most dramatic landscapes in India, from the rhododendron-clad slopes of the Singalila Range to the pristine glacial lakes such as Tsomgo Lake and Gurudongmar Lake. The crown jewel of Sikkim's natural beauty is undoubtedly the majestic Kangchenjunga, the third highest mountain in the world, which towers over the state and is revered by the local people as a protective deity. The mountain's presence is felt across Sikkim, influencing local culture and spiritual life.

Sikkim's biodiversity is also notable, with its forests home to a myriad of plant and animal species that thrive in both the tropical and temperate zones. The state's protected areas, such as the Khangchendzonga National Park, serve as sanctuaries for wildlife, including the snow leopard, red panda, and Himalayan tahr, among others. These areas are critical not just for conservation purposes but also for research and education about the Himalayan environment and its global ecological significance.

However, the balance between development and conservation is a continual challenge for Sikkim. While its organic and eco-tourism initiatives have brought numerous benefits, they also come with the pressures of managing increased tourist footfall and maintaining the integrity of its natural and cultural resources. The state's approach to these challenges is closely watched as a model by other regions aiming to combine ecological sustainability with economic growth.

Sikkim represents a remarkable convergence of ecological responsibility and natural beauty. The state's commitment to organic farming is a reflection of a broader ethos of respect for nature, which is evident in every aspect of life in Sikkim. From the green terraces of its farms to the snowy peaks of its northern borders, Sikkim offers a vision of what is possible when a community is committed to living in harmony with its environment. This commitment has not only preserved the breathtaking landscapes of Sikkim but has also ensured that they continue to inspire and sustain future generations. As Sikkim continues to develop, it holds onto its core values of sustainability and harmony, offering lessons for the world on the integration of human aspirations with environmental stewardship.

ᠵᠵᠵ

"The sacred city of Varanasi, where the river meets the soul, witnesses life and death on its ghats, each a profound testament to the eternal cycles of existence."

▷▷▷

THIRTEEN

ASSAM: THE TEA GARDENS AND TRANQUIL BRAHMAPUTRA

Assam, located in the verdant northeast of India, is a realm where the rhythms of nature dictate the pace of life. The state is renowned for its sprawling tea gardens and the majestic Brahmaputra River, which together form the backbone of its economy and cultural identity. These elements, intertwined with the daily lives of the Assamese people, showcase a landscape that is as economically significant as it is breathtakingly beautiful.

The Brahmaputra River, often referred to as the lifeblood of Assam, is one of the major rivers in the world. Originating from the Angsi Glacier in Tibet, the river enters India in Arunachal Pradesh and flows through Assam before descending into Bangladesh. In Assam, the Brahmaputra is more than just a river; it is a source of sustenance, a means of transport, and a spiritual heartland for the local people. Its banks are lined with lush greenery and fertile plains that support agriculture, which sustains the rural economy.

The river is central to Assamese culture, influencing the literature, music, and festivals of the region. It is revered as a nurturing mother, providing and protecting in equal measure.

The annual flood cycle of the Brahmaputra, while often causing widespread disruption, is also crucial for replenishing the soil fertility of the region. This natural phenomenon brings rich silt and organic matter that enhance the agricultural lands along its banks, particularly benefiting the tea plantations that are synonymous with Assam. However, these floods can also lead to severe loss of life and property, prompting extensive flood management efforts, including embankments and controlled diversions.

Tea production in Assam is one of the most palpable manifestations of the state's economic activities, with Assam Tea being renowned worldwide for its robust flavor and bright color. The tea gardens of Assam, which date back to the mid-19th century when the British colonial administration established tea plantations, cover vast expanses of land, particularly in the Upper Assam region. These gardens are not merely agricultural sites; they are part of the state's heritage and play a critical role in the socio-economic fabric of Assam.

Working in the tea gardens involves meticulous skills in planting, pruning, and picking the tea leaves, practices that have been refined over generations. The laborers, often women, are seen as custodians of this tradition, their expert hands picking the tea leaves with precision that ensures the high quality of Assam tea. The tea industry also supports numerous ancillary industries, including transport, packaging, and export services, contributing significantly to Assam's economy.

Moreover, Assam tea is deeply integrated into the social life of the state. Chai, or tea, is a staple beverage for the Assamese people, consumed several times a day and offered to guests as a sign of hospitality. The social ritual of drinking tea, often accompanied by local snacks, is a moment of relaxation and community bonding.

Beyond its economic impact, the tea gardens are also ecological habitats. They support a variety of flora and fauna, providing green cover that is beneficial for the environment. Efforts are being made to promote sustainable practices within the tea industry to ensure that this green cover is not only maintained but enhanced.

However, challenges such as climate change, labor issues, and market fluctuations impact the tea industry. The changing patterns of rainfall and temperature, attributed to global climate change, are affecting tea production, with shifts in the quality and quantity of the yield. Furthermore, the welfare of tea garden workers and their families, including issues related to wages, health, and education, are of critical concern. Addressing these challenges requires a coordinated approach involving government policies, industry practices, and community engagement.

The Brahmaputra and the tea gardens are not just the economic engines of Assam but are also emblematic of the state's natural beauty and cultural richness. They shape the landscape, define the rhythms of rural life, and influence the social fabric of the region. As Assam navigates the complexities of modern development and environmental conservation, the interplay between these natural resources will continue to be central to its identity and prosperity. Assam's future, intertwined with the fate of its mighty river and lush tea gardens, remains a story of balance between harnessing resources and preserving the natural environment that defines this unique part of India.

ᑭᑭᑭ

"In the palaces of Mysore, history walks through opulent halls, each arch and artifact narrating tales of royal grandeur and the whispers of bygone eras."

❦❦❦

FOURTEEN

ODISHA: THE DANCE OF NATURE AND DEVOTION

Odisha, a state on the eastern coast of India, is a region where the natural world and deep-seated devotion dance in harmony. Known for its lush landscapes, pristine beaches, and rich cultural heritage, Odisha represents a unique blend of natural beauty and spiritual richness. This state, with its diverse ecosystems ranging from dense forests and fertile plains to a long, unspoiled coastline, offers a panorama of nature that is as varied as it is stunning. Coupled with this natural splendor is a tradition of spirituality and cultural expressions that permeate every aspect of life in Odisha.

The landscapes of Odisha are a testament to the state's geographical diversity. The Eastern Ghats run through Odisha, presenting a terrain that is rugged yet rich with biodiversity. These hills are home to numerous tribes whose lifestyles and traditions have remained closely tied to the natural environment. The forests in these areas are dense and are sanctuaries for a wide range of flora and fauna, contributing significantly to India's biodiversity. Simlipal National Park, one of the largest wildlife sanctuaries in India, lies in this region and is part of the UNESCO World Network of Biosphere Reserves. It is a haven for majestic tigers, beautiful orchids, and a myriad of other species, all thriving in a complex ecological web that is meticulously preserved.

Moving from the hills to the coast, Odisha's beaches are among the most serene and beautiful in India. The coastline stretches for over 480 kilometers, featuring beaches like Puri, Gopalpur, and Chandipur. These are not just natural wonders but also centers of activity and festivity, especially during the annual Rath Yatra in Puri. The Puri Beach hosts millions of devotees who participate in this grand chariot festival, which is a spectacle of devotion and celebration. The festival is deeply intertwined with the Jagannath Temple, a revered site that draws visitors from across the globe. The temple's elaborate rituals and the vibrant procession of the Rath Yatra are integral to the spiritual life of the people and reflect a culture that venerates nature and divinity equally.

Alongside its natural and spiritual allure, Odisha is also celebrated for its rich culinary traditions, notably its spices. The state's cuisine is a rich tapestry of flavors, with dishes that are both nuanced and bold. Spices such as turmeric, mustard, and cumin are staples in the Odishan kitchen, used not only for their flavors but also for their health benefits. These spices are locally grown, benefiting from the fertile soils and the moist climate of the region, which enhance their aroma and potency. Markets in Odisha, from the capital Bhubaneswar to smaller towns, are vibrant with the colors and scents of these spices, alongside fresh vegetables, fruits, and other local produce.

The integration of spices into the diet is seen in numerous traditional dishes such as Pakhala (fermented rice), which is often seasoned with mustard seeds and curry leaves, and Pithas (sweet or savory cakes) that are subtly flavored with cardamom and other spices. These dishes are not merely meals but are part of the rituals and celebrations that mark the Odishan calendar, reflecting the state's philosophy of food as a means to nourish both body and spirit.

Odisha's commitment to preserving its natural and cultural heritage is evident in its approach to tourism and development. Efforts are made to promote sustainable tourism that respects the natural environment and enhances the social and economic well-being of local communities. This includes conserving its forests, protecting its wildlife, and maintaining the cleanliness and sanctity of its beaches and temples.

However, the challenges of environmental conservation and cultural preservation are significant. Balancing economic development with environmental sustainability requires careful planning and community involvement. Initiatives to educate and engage local populations in conservation efforts are crucial, as is the promotion of practices that ensure the long-term health of Odisha's natural resources.

Odisha is a land where nature and devotion create a symphony of experiences that are profoundly moving and deeply enriching. From the dance of its tribal cultures in the forests of the Eastern Ghats to the rhythmic waves on its sandy shores, from the vibrant hues of its spice markets to the solemn rituals of its temples, Odisha offers a journey through landscapes that are both externally beautiful and spiritually significant. As Odisha continues to navigate the path of modernization, it holds tight to the threads of tradition and nature, weaving a future that respects its past while embracing the new, ensuring that the dance of nature and devotion continues to thrive in this enchanting corner of India.

ppp

"The snows of Kashmir do more than just cloak the mountains; they blanket centuries of poetry, conflict, and the dreams of peace."

❧❧❧

FIFTEEN

CHHATTISGARH: THE UNTOUCHED NATURAL PARADISE

Chhattisgarh, often described as an untouched natural paradise, is one of India's most verdant states, with dense forests covering a large part of its territory. These vast stretches of wilderness are not only significant for their ecological value but also for the cultural heritage they sustain. The state is home to a diverse array of tribal communities, each with its own unique traditions and ways of life that are closely intertwined with the natural environment. This symbiotic relationship between the land and its people is a defining characteristic of Chhattisgarh, making it a fascinating study of biodiversity and cultural richness.

The forests of Chhattisgarh are some of the most extensive in India, constituting about 44% of the state's land area. These forests range from tropical moist deciduous in the northern and central areas to tropical dry deciduous in the southern and eastern parts. Such diversity in flora is accompanied by an equally diverse fauna, making these forests a biodiversity hotspot. Among the notable national parks and wildlife sanctuaries in Chhattisgarh are the

Achanakmar Wildlife Sanctuary, known for its populations of tigers, leopards, and gaurs, and the Kanger Valley National Park, famous for its scenic beauty and the rare Bastar hill myna.

The state's commitment to preserving its natural heritage is evident in its conservation practices and the establishment of several protected areas. These efforts are crucial not only for protecting the flora and fauna but also for maintaining the ecological balance of the region. The lush green cover helps in regulating the climate, preserving soil fertility, and sustaining the water cycles — essential elements for life in and around these areas.

The tribes of Chhattisgarh, such as the Gond, Baiga, and Korba, have lived in harmony with these forests for centuries. Their lives are deeply rooted in the ecosystem they inhabit. They depend on the forests for food, medicine, and materials for building and handicrafts, which are central to their economic and social practices. The tribal communities have an intricate knowledge of the medicinal properties of various plants, and this traditional knowledge is invaluable for both healthcare and the conservation of these species. Their cultural practices, including festivals, dances, and rituals, reflect their respect and reverence for nature, and many such celebrations are directly linked to agricultural cycles and seasonal changes.

Moreover, the unique biodiversity of Chhattisgarh's forests includes not only wildlife but also numerous plant species that are of great ecological and medicinal value. The state is particularly renowned for its rich variety of medicinal plants, and it hosts several plant species that are rare and endangered. This botanical wealth not only supports the local ecosystems but also provides opportunities for scientific research and pharmaceutical development.

However, the isolation and purity of Chhattisgarh's natural environments also face significant challenges. Deforestation, mining activities, and industrialization threaten the ecological balance and the traditional lifestyle of tribal communities. These activities risk fragmenting the habitats of numerous species and may lead to conflicts over land and resources. The challenge for Chhattisgarh is to find a balance between economic development and environmental sustainability. Efforts to empower local communities through sustainable practices and ecotourism are seen as vital steps in preserving both the natural environment and the cultural heritage of the tribes.

In response to these challenges, various initiatives aimed at promoting sustainable development and community-based conservation have been implemented. These include programs to educate and involve local communities in wildlife protection efforts and the promotion of sustainable agricultural practices that are compatible with the conservation of forests. The government and several NGOs also work towards enhancing the livelihoods of tribal populations while ensuring the protection of their cultural and environmental resources.

Chhattisgarh's untouched natural paradise, with its dense forests, diverse tribes, and unique biodiversity, represents a critical part of India's natural and cultural heritage. The state exemplifies how biodiversity can coexist with cultural richness, providing a blueprint for conservation and sustainable development. As Chhattisgarh navigates the complexities of modernization and environmental preservation, its forests and tribes continue to play a crucial role in maintaining the ecological health of the region. The ongoing efforts to protect this rich natural heritage ensure that Chhattisgarh remains a beacon for environmentalists and cultural anthropologists alike, showcasing the enduring beauty and resilience of nature and humanity.

ppp

"Chhattisgarh's forests are the lungs of the land,
breathing life into the tribes and wildlife that
coexist in this splendid isolation."

❦❦❦

SIXTEEN

MAHARASHTRA: THE SAHYADRIS AND SPICES

Maharashtra, a state of striking contrasts and immense diversity, stretches from the stunning Sahyadri ranges of the Western Ghats to the vast Arabian Sea coastline, encapsulating an array of ecosystems and cultures within its borders. It is a land where ancient traditions merge seamlessly with modernity, particularly visible in its bustling cities, majestic landscapes, and the vibrant spice markets that are a testament to its rich culinary heritage.

The Western Ghats, known locally as the Sahyadris, form a significant part of Maharashtra's topographical identity. This mountain range is not only renowned for its breathtaking natural beauty and panoramic landscapes but also for its biological diversity. The Ghats are recognized as a UNESCO World Heritage Site and are one of the world's eight "hottest hotspots" of biological diversity. These ranges are home to thousands of species of flora and fauna, many of which are endemic to the region. The dense forests that carpet the hills are interrupted only by streams and waterfalls, creating a landscape that is as picturesque as it is ecologically vital.

The Sahyadris play a crucial role in influencing the climate of the region, acting as a barrier that traps the monsoon winds, thereby causing heavy rainfall in the area. This phenomenon not only sustains the lush greenery of the region but also feeds the rivers that are lifelines to the rural and urban areas downstream. Additionally, the Ghats are the source of several important rivers like the Godavari and Krishna, which support the agriculture of the entire region, demonstrating the interconnectivity of natural systems that sustain the state.

Descending from the heights of the Western Ghats to the extensive coastline along the Arabian Sea, Maharashtra's beaches are as diverse as they are scenic. From the popular sands of Girgaum in Mumbai to the serene stretches in Ratnagiri and the fortified coastline of Alibaug, these coastal areas are integral to the cultural and economic fabric of the state. The coast is dotted with ancient forts, quaint fishing villages, and modern ports, each telling stories of Maharashtra's maritime heritage. The fisheries along this coast are a vital part of the state's economy, and the daily life of the coastal communities is deeply intertwined with the sea.

One cannot discuss Maharashtra without mentioning its vibrant spice markets, especially those in Mumbai, the state's capital and the financial hub of India. Mumbai's spice markets, such as those in Crawford Market and the lanes of Masjid Bunder, are bustling with activity, where the air is thick with the aroma of spices like turmeric, cumin, coriander, and the Mumbai special, the fiery 'Lalbaug' chili powder. These markets are not just commercial hubs but are also cultural landmarks that showcase the diversity of Maharashtra's culinary practices.

The spices found in these markets are used in a variety of Maharashtrian dishes, from the coastal seafood curries to the robust meat preparations of the interior regions. Spices are used not just for their flavors but also for their health benefits, playing a significant role in both the state's cuisine and its traditional medicine. Maharashtrian cuisine, with its array of fiercely spicy and mildly flavored dishes, offers a gastronomic mirror to the state's diverse cultural tapestry, influenced by various ethnic communities and historical interactions.

Moreover, the spice trade in Maharashtra is not a new phenomenon but has historical roots that go back centuries, linking the region to global trade networks. The ports along the Maharashtra coast have been gateways for the import and export of spices, among other goods, facilitating cultural exchanges that have enriched local traditions. Today, these spice markets are not only crucial for the local economy but also serve as attractions that draw tourists and food enthusiasts from across the world, eager to experience the flavors and stories that these spices carry.

However, the state faces the challenge of balancing development and conservation, especially in preserving the ecological sanctity of the Western Ghats and the sustainability of the coastal and marine environments. Urbanization and industrialization pose significant threats to these natural habitats, necessitating concerted conservation efforts. Initiatives aimed at promoting sustainable tourism and responsible resource management are critical in ensuring that Maharashtra's natural and cultural heritage is preserved for future generations.

Maharashtra is a mosaic of landscapes and cultures, where the rugged beauty of the Sahyadris and the tranquil expanses of its coastline create a backdrop for the vibrant life of its cities and the aromatic bustle of its spice markets. This interplay of natural beauty, cultural richness, and historical depth makes Maharashtra a microcosm of India's diversity, offering insights into the past and lessons for the future. As the state continues to navigate the complexities of growth and conservation, the legacy of its mountains, coasts, and spices stands as a reminder of the treasures that need protecting in this dynamic region.

ϷϷϷ

"The waves of the Arabian Sea, as they touch the
shores of Maharashtra, bring with them stories
from distant lands, told with the salt of the sea."

▷▷▷

SEVENTEEN
GOA: SAND, SPICES, AND SERENITY

Goa, a small yet vibrant state on the western coast of India, is a place where the azure waters of the Arabian Sea meet the shore, lined with swaying coconut palms and sun-drenched beaches. Known for its scenic beauty, laid-back lifestyle, and rich cultural tapestry, Goa is a unique blend of Indian and Portuguese influences, which is reflected in everything from its architectural designs to its culinary flavors and social customs.

The Portuguese first arrived in Goa in the early 16th century and ruled for over 450 years, leaving an indelible mark on the state's cultural landscape. This prolonged contact has resulted in a distinctive Goan identity that is a synthesis of Eastern and Western traditions. Architecturally, Goa is renowned for its stunning churches, particularly the Basilica of Bom Jesus which houses the remains of St. Francis Xavier and is a UNESCO World Heritage Site. These majestic structures are characterized by their ornate decoration and baroque architecture, which stand in contrast yet in harmony with the more traditional and modest Hindu temples scattered throughout the state.

This cultural fusion is most deliciously evident in Goan cuisine, which is a flavorful blend of Portuguese and local Indian cooking techniques and ingredients. Goan food is richly layered with spices that are both locally grown and imported, which have been integrated into the culinary traditions brought by the Portuguese. Dishes such as Vindaloo, originally from Portugal but adapted to local tastes with the addition of palm vinegar, garlic, and Kashmiri chili, embody this melding of cultures. Similarly, Xacuti and Cafreal reflect the unique syncretism of Goan cuisine, using spices like nutmeg, cloves, and cardamom that are intensively cultivated in the region along with local ingredients like coconut and kokum.

Goa's spice farms are another attraction, offering a glimpse into the state's agricultural practices and the variety of spices that are grown, including black pepper, vanilla, and cinnamon. These spice farms not only allow visitors to learn about spice cultivation but also play a crucial role in sustaining the local economy. Tourists can walk through aromatic spice plantations, which offer an immersive experience into the world of spices, from growing and harvesting to the drying and grinding processes.

The serene and beautiful beaches of Goa are perhaps its most famous attractions, drawing millions of tourists from across the globe each year. From the bustling beaches of Calangute and Baga, where the nightlife and water sports thrive, to the quieter southern shores like Palolem and Agonda, each beach has its own character and charm. These coastal stretches are places where people from various walks of life come together to relax, celebrate, and enjoy the natural beauty of the sea.

Beyond the physical allure, the beaches of Goa are also cultural hotspots. The annual Goa Carnival, an event that dates back to the Portuguese era, is a vibrant celebration featuring parades, music, dancing, and the traditional float parade. This festival, along with the famous Sunburn music festival, highlights the cosmopolitan nature of Goa, where diverse cultural influences and modern entertainment coalesce.

However, the popularity of Goa as a tourist destination also brings challenges, particularly to its ecological and cultural environment. Issues such as coastal erosion, the overdevelopment of tourist facilities, and the impact of tourism on local communities are areas of concern. The state government and various NGOs are actively working to promote sustainable tourism practices that minimize environmental impact while enhancing the visitor experience.

Goa represents a unique cultural and natural paradise where the legacies of its Portuguese past blend seamlessly with traditional Indian elements. From its spice-laden cuisine to the architectural gems and the splendid beaches, Goa offers a distinctive experience that is both intoxicating and serene. It is a place where history is alive in every alley and corner, where the music of the past plays in harmony with the rhythms of modern life, and where every sunset brings with it a promise of continued coexistence and mutual respect between the various cultures that have come to call this state their home. As Goa continues to navigate the challenges of modernity and tradition, it remains a testament to the enduring appeal of a truly global cultural synthesis.

"Odisha's dance forms, from the classical to the tribal, are a movement of color and emotion, painting stories in the air with every turn and twirl."

▷▷▷

EIGHTEEN

KARNATAKA: FROM COFFEE ESTATES TO COASTAL DELIGHTS

Karnataka, a state in the southwestern region of India, is a land of dramatic contrasts and diverse landscapes. From the verdant coffee estates nestled in its hilly regions to the rugged beauty of the Western Ghats and the serene expanse of its coastal belt, Karnataka offers a rich tapestry of natural and cultural experiences. This diversity not only makes Karnataka a unique destination for travelers but also reflects the ecological and agricultural richness that sustains its local populations and economies.

The journey through Karnataka's landscapes can begin in the lush, mist-covered hills of the Western Ghats, known locally as the Sahyadris. This mountain range is a UNESCO World Heritage Site and one of the eight "hottest hotspots" of biological diversity in the world. The Ghats traverse the length of Karnataka, providing a home to thousands of species of flora and fauna, many of which are endemic to this region. The dense forests of the Ghats are interspersed with hidden waterfalls, deep valleys, and high peaks, offering breathtaking views and a haven for trekkers and nature lovers. The ecological significance of the Western Ghats extends beyond its biodiversity; it plays a crucial role in influencing the climate of the region, acting as a barrier that intercepts the monsoon winds and facilitates the heavy rainfall that feeds the rivers and streams flowing through the state.

Ascending from the lush greenery of the lower Western Ghats, one reaches the coffee plantations of Coorg and Chikmagalur, areas synonymous with coffee cultivation in India. Karnataka is one of the largest coffee-producing states in the country, with its coffee renowned for its high quality and distinctive flavor, attributed to the unique soil and climatic conditions of the region. The coffee estates here are not just agricultural lands; they are part of Karnataka's heritage and a key attraction for agro-tourism. These estates often resemble vast gardens with neatly lined coffee bushes interspersed with spices like pepper and cardamom, which provide additional income to the farmers. Tourists visiting these estates can experience the entire process of coffee production, from picking and drying to roasting and grinding, offering insight into the intricacies of coffee farming.

The experience of the coffee plantations reflects a larger agricultural tradition in Karnataka, which is characterized by a blend of traditional practices and modern innovations. This tradition ensures the preservation of the ecological balance while meeting the economic needs of the local communities. The plantations are also a reflection of the cultural heritage of Karnataka, with estate homes and community spaces that are often centuries old, holding stories of the region's colonial past and its evolution over time.

Moving from the interior landscapes to the coastal regions of Karnataka, the scenery shifts dramatically. The state's coastline stretches over 300 kilometers along the Arabian Sea, featuring pristine beaches, scenic backwaters, and historic port towns like

Mangalore and Karwar. These coastal areas are not only popular for their natural beauty but also for their rich culinary traditions, which are distinctly different from the interior parts of the state. Seafood is a staple here, with dishes flavored with coconut and kokum, a sour fruit that is a hallmark of coastal Karnataka cuisine.

The coastal regions also hold significant economic and historical importance. The ports along the Karnataka coast have been centers of maritime trade for centuries, facilitating cultural exchanges and contributing to the state's prosperity. Historical sites along the coast, such as the ancient temples and forts, tell the tales of dynasties like the Vijayanagara Empire and colonial powers that shaped the region's history.

However, the diverse landscapes of Karnataka, from its coffee estates to the coastal areas, face challenges related to environmental conservation and sustainable development. The pressures of tourism, urbanization, and climate change pose threats to the delicate ecosystems of the Western Ghats and the coastal regions. Initiatives aimed at promoting eco-tourism and sustainable agricultural practices are crucial in preserving these landscapes for future generations.

Karnataka's landscapes, from the aromatic coffee estates to the tranquil coastal delights, offer a journey through a state that is as varied in its geography as it is in its cultural expressions. These landscapes not only define the physical character of Karnataka but also shape the lives, economies, and traditions of its people. As Karnataka continues to develop and modernize, the challenge lies in maintaining the balance between preserving its natural beauty and cultural heritage and embracing the opportunities of the future. This balance is key to ensuring that Karnataka remains a vibrant and sustainable state, true to its roots yet open to the world.

ppp

"*Punjab's fields, stretching under sweeping skies, are not merely plots of land but the very fabric of community, woven tight with the strands of shared toil.*"

❧❧❧

NINETEEN

KERALA: GOD'S OWN COUNTRY

Kerala, aptly dubbed "God's Own Country," is a testament to the unrivaled beauty and serenity that nature can offer. Located on the southwestern coast of India, this state is a mosaic of stunning landscapes, from the tranquil backwaters and lush spice gardens to the verdant greenery that drapes itself across the region. Kerala's unique geography and the equitable climate contribute to its rich biodiversity and the cultivation of various spices that have made it a key player in the global spice trade for centuries.

The backwaters of Kerala are perhaps the most iconic feature of the state's landscape. This intricate network of interconnected canals, rivers, lakes, and inlets stretches across the coast of Kerala, forming more than 900 kilometers of waterways. These backwaters are not only a vital aspect of the region's ecosystem but also a major tourist attraction, offering serene boat rides on houseboats (Kettuvallams) that glide through the tranquil waters, providing a glimpse into the rural life of Kerala. Villages along the backwaters thrive on a lifestyle that has remained largely unchanged over the centuries, with local inhabitants engaging in traditional fishing, coconut harvesting, and rice farming. The tranquility of the backwaters is juxtaposed with the bustling activity of the locals, offering a picturesque scene of Kerala's vibrant yet laid-back rural life.

The lush greenery of Kerala is largely due to its climate, which features heavy monsoonal rains that sustain the diverse flora and fauna of the region. This green landscape is home to a number of wildlife sanctuaries and national parks, including Periyar Wildlife Sanctuary, renowned for its elephant populations and the elusive Bengal tiger. Beyond its ecological value, the forested areas of Kerala are a hotbed for gathering and cultivating a range of spices that are integral to both the cuisine and economy of the state.

Kerala's spice gardens are as varied as they are prolific. The region's hills, particularly in places like Munnar and Thekkady, are dotted with plantations where cardamom, pepper, vanilla, cinnamon, and nutmeg are grown. These spices have historically driven the economy of Kerala, drawing traders from across the world and giving the region a prominent place on the spice map of the world. The spice gardens themselves are a draw for tourists and botanists alike, who come to wander among the fragrant greenery and learn about the cultivation processes that produce some of the world's most sought-after spices.

Moreover, the culture of Kerala is deeply influenced by its relationship with the natural environment. The traditional architecture, seen in the ancient homes and temples throughout the state, often incorporates local materials like coconut timber, mud, and laterite stone, which naturally regulate air circulation and temperature, suited perfectly to the humid climate. Rituals and festivals in Kerala, too, celebrate the bounty of the land and water. One of the most spectacular of these is the annual snake boat race in Alappuzha, where teams of rowers cut through the backwaters in long, slender boats, competing in a vibrant and spirited display of community and tradition.

However, the very elements that make Kerala a paradise also pose challenges. The state is prone to environmental hazards such as floods and landslides, exacerbated by climate change and deforestation. The delicate balance of ecosystems in the backwaters and the Western Ghats is susceptible to disruptions from unchecked tourist activity and industrial development. Efforts to promote sustainable tourism and agriculture are vital to maintaining Kerala's natural beauty and ecological health.

Kerala embodies a unique blend of natural beauty, cultural richness, and historical significance, making it truly deserving of its moniker, God's Own Country. From the quiet majesty of the backwaters to the aromatic allure of its spice gardens and the lush density of its green landscapes, Kerala offers a profound experience of nature's bounty and the harmonious ways in which human cultures can coexist with it. As Kerala continues to navigate the challenges of conservation and development, it remains a symbol of how natural beauty can define a region's identity and inspire both its residents and visitors to preserve its legacy for generations to come.

❧❧❧

"Kerala's spice gardens are like nature's treasure chests, each leaf and seed a nugget of gold, enriching dishes with more than just flavor but centuries of heritage."

❧❧❧

TWENTY

Tamil Nadu to Kanyakumari: A Cultural Mosaic

Tamil Nadu, located in the southernmost part of India, is a state steeped in history, culture, and tradition. As one travels from the bustling cities and majestic temples of Tamil Nadu to the serene southern tip at Kanyakumari, there unfolds a vivid tapestry of cultural and natural landscapes that embody the rich diversity of the region. This journey through Tamil Nadu to Kanyakumari offers a profound insight into the soul of South India, showcasing a vibrant cultural mosaic that spans millennia and continues to thrive in the modern age.

Tamil Nadu is renowned for its architectural marvels, particularly the towering, intricately carved temples which are not just places of worship but also epitomes of art and engineering. These temples, many of which are UNESCO World Heritage Sites, are scattered across the state, from the grand Brihadeeswarar Temple in Thanjavur to the ornate Meenakshi Temple in Madurai. Each temple narrates stories from Hindu epics, rendered in stone and imbued with the devotional spirit of centuries. The Dravidian style of architecture, characterized by its towering gopurams (gateway towers) and detailed sculptural work, draws not only the faithful but also art historians and tourists from around the world.

Beyond their religious significance, these temples are hubs of cultural activity, hosting an array of festivals throughout the year. Festivals like Pongal, the harvest festival, and Navaratri, a celebration of the goddess Durga, are marked by vibrant rituals, traditional music, and dance performances that reflect the rich cultural heritage of Tamil Nadu. These celebrations are not just about worship but also about community bonding, where people from various walks of life come together to celebrate their traditions and shared histories.

The journey through Tamil Nadu is also a journey through its rich literary tradition, which is one of the oldest in the world. Tamil literature, with its classical roots stretching back over two millennia, continues to influence the social and cultural life of the state. The works of Sangam literature, composed between 300 BCE and 300 CE, are still celebrated for their poetic excellence and profound humanity, offering insights into the ancient Tamil way of life, their love for the land, and their complex social structures.

As one travels further south to the tip of the Indian subcontinent, the landscape shifts to the coastal beauty of Kanyakumari. This town, named after the virgin goddess Kanyakumari, is famed for its spectacular sunrises and sunsets, especially at the confluence of the Arabian Sea, Indian Ocean, and the Bay of Bengal. The iconic Vivekananda Rock Memorial, situated on a small island off the coast, marks the spot where Swami Vivekananda meditated and is a symbol of spiritual unity and peace. This serene spot offers panoramic views of the vast ocean and serves as a pilgrimage site for those seeking spiritual solace.

Kanyakumari is not just a geographic endpoint; it is a cultural amalgam where one can see the confluence of various cultural influences—from the indigenous Dravidian to the colonial Portuguese. The town's architecture, cuisine, and customs reflect this blend, making it a microcosm of the cultural synthesis that characterizes much of Tamil Nadu.

However, the region's ecological and cultural landscapes face challenges from urbanization and the pressures of tourism. The delicate coastal ecosystems of Kanyakumari and the ancient temples across Tamil Nadu require careful conservation to preserve their natural beauty and historical significance. Efforts to promote sustainable tourism and environmental stewardship are crucial in ensuring that these cultural landmarks continue to inspire awe and reverence for generations to come.

The journey from Tamil Nadu to Kanyakumari encapsulates a diverse cultural experience, rich in history, art, and spirituality. From the grandeur of its temples to the serene beauty of its southern coast, this region offers a unique window into the soul of South India. The enduring traditions, architectural wonders, and poetic legacies of Tamil Nadu, culminating in the picturesque landscapes of Kanyakumari, provide a fitting finale to a journey through a land where the past and present coalesce into a vibrant tapestry of human endeavor and natural beauty. As Tamil Nadu continues to navigate the complexities of preserving its cultural and natural heritage, it remains a beacon of cultural richness and ecological diversity, embodying the timeless spirit of India.

"In the tranquility of Himachal's hill stations, one finds a quietude that is as profound as the valleys are deep; here, the horizon is not just seen but felt."

❥❥❥

TWENTY-ONE
SUMMARY: A JOURNEY THROUGH INDIA'S RICH TAPESTRY

This book has taken readers on an enriching journey through India, exploring the diverse landscapes, cultures, and traditions that define this vast country. From the northern reaches of Kashmir to the southern tip of Kanyakumari, each chapter has delved into the unique aspects of different states, weaving a comprehensive tapestry of India's ecological, cultural, and historical richness.

Kashmir, described as paradise on Earth, is celebrated for its breathtaking landscapes and rich traditions, including the cultivation of saffron. The serene beauty of the Dal Lake and the vibrant colors of the saffron fields exemplify the natural and cultural wealth of the region.

Punjab, the land of the five rivers, is known for its fertile plains and robust agricultural practices. The Golden Temple in Amritsar stands as a symbol of spiritual solace and communal harmony, embodying the vibrant cultural life of the state.

Himachal Pradesh offers a glimpse into the tranquil hill stations and lush orchards, where traditional lifestyles blend seamlessly with the natural surroundings. The spiritual sites and scenic beauty of places like Shimla and Manali attract visitors seeking both adventure and peace.

Uttarakhand, revered for its sacred sites and the pristine beauty of the Himalayas, serves as a focal point for pilgrims and nature lovers alike. The convergence of the Ganges and Yamuna at Haridwar represents both a spiritual junction and a natural spectacle.

Delhi, the capital city, presents a blend of historical richness and modern dynamism. The architectural marvels, ranging from the Mughal-era Red Fort to the colonial India Gate, narrate the city's layered history.

Madhya Pradesh, the heart of India, is known for its dense forests and wildlife sanctuaries. The state's rich tribal culture and historical sites like the Buddhist stupas at Sanchi offer insights into its ancient civilizations.

Gujarat tells a story of cultural diversity and economic vibrancy, from the legendary kite festival in Ahmedabad to the serene Gir Forest, home to the Asiatic lion.

Rajasthan brings to life the tales of Rajput valor and the architectural grandeur of its palaces and forts. The vivid colors of Jaipur's markets and the desert landscapes of Jaisalmer capture the essence of this historic state.

Uttar Pradesh is characterized by its religious significance and the majestic flow of the Ganges. The cultural and religious festivities in Varanasi and the historical grandeur of Agra, featuring the Taj

Mahal, showcase the state's profound cultural heritage.

Bihar, with its Buddhist pilgrimage sites and ancient universities like Nalanda, provides a window into India's historical depth and spiritual teachings.

West Bengal is distinguished by its intellectual heritage and vibrant arts scene, epitomized by Kolkata, a city of poets and scholars. The Sunderbans mangrove forests and the Darjeeling tea gardens highlight the state's natural diversity.

Sikkim stands out for its organic farming initiatives and stunning natural reserves, which are significant for conservation efforts and eco-tourism.

Assam is synonymous with its lush tea gardens and the mighty Brahmaputra River, which plays a central role in agriculture and local folklore.

Odisha showcases a rich tapestry of tribal culture, historic temples, and maritime heritage, with the Jagannath Temple in Puri being a major religious site.

Chhattisgarh offers a look into India's untouched natural beauty and the tribal traditions that are closely linked with the state's forests and biodiversity.

Maharashtra combines the grandeur of the Western Ghats with the bustling city life of Mumbai, offering everything from hill forts to coastal beaches.

Goa, with its sandy beaches, historical Portuguese architecture, and vibrant nightlife, serves as a tropical haven for visitors from around the world.

Karnataka captures the essence of its coffee plantations and ancient ruins, while also hosting modern technological hubs like Bengaluru.

Kerala, described as God's Own Country, is renowned for its backwaters, spice gardens, and the harmonious coexistence of nature and culture.

Tamil Nadu is celebrated for its Dravidian architecture, rich culinary traditions, and the classical arts, culminating in the picturesque landscapes of Kanyakumari.

This journey through India illustrates the sheer diversity and richness of the Indian subcontinent. Each state not only presents its own set of natural wonders, cultural richness, and historical significance but also contributes to the complex mosaic that is India. The ongoing challenge for India lies in balancing modern development with the preservation of its cultural heritage and natural environments. As India continues to evolve, it remains a land of unparalleled diversity and enduring traditions, promising endless exploration and discovery for both residents and visitors alike.

ᐯᐯᐯ

Citation And References

This book represents the culmination of extensive research and meticulous analysis, incorporating a diverse range of sources, including numerous books, scholarly studies, and personal experiences. Additionally, I have scoured various websites to gather relevant information and data essential for the compilation of this work. I have taken every precaution to ensure the accuracy of the information presented and have diligently cited all sources to acknowledge their contributions.

Despite these efforts, the possibility of inadvertent errors remains. I deeply value the insights of my readers and appreciate any feedback that can help identify and rectify such inaccuracies. I encourage you to bring any discrepancies to my attention.

Your feedback is not only welcome but crucial, as it will aid in correcting current editions and enhancing the content of future ones. I am committed to maintaining the highest standards of accuracy and reliability in my work and thank you for your support and understanding.

Additionally, I firmly uphold the principle of freedom of speech and expression as guaranteed under Article 19(1)(a) of the Constitution of India, and I respect the diverse viewpoints and expressions of all readers.

ÞÞÞ

Other Books Of The Author

1. Empowering Minds: A Journey into Women's Self-Discovery and Power
2. The Dynamics of Motivation: Catalyzing Thought into Action
3. Meditation and Mental Well Being: The Path to Inner Peace and Clarity
4. The Psychology of Child Education: Nurturing Future Generations
5. Ethical Enlightenment: A Modern Guide to Living with Integrity
6. Voices of Empowerment: Stories of Women Rising Against Odds
7. Social Psychology in Everyday Life: Understanding Human Connections
8. The Essence of Motivational Speaking: Inspiring Change in Others
9. Balancing Acts: Women, Work, and the Will to Lead
10. Guiding with Grace: Raising Children with Compassion and Awareness
11. The Power of Positive Aging: Embracing Life After Fifty
12. Building Resilient Communities: Social Work in Action
13. The Ethical Educator: Principles for Teaching and Learning
14. From Insight to Impact: Social Psychology for a Better World
15. The Ethics of Empathy: A Guide to Ethical Living
16. The Science of Empowering the Self: Navigating Life's Challenges with Psychological Wisdom
17. The Mindful Conscious Leader: Meditation Techniques for Modern Management
18. Pioneering Spirit: Women's Pathways to Leadership and Empowerment
19. Feeling to Healing: The Role of Emotional Intelligence in Child Development
20. Transformative Talks and Words of Inspiration: Insights into Motivational Oratory

ॐॐॐ

Contact

Dr. Minakshi Bansal
Social Activist
Ahmedabad, Gujarat, Bharat
minakshiindiag20@yahoo.com

❥❥❥

|| LOKAHA SAMASTHAHA SUKHINO BHAVANTU ||

• 131 •